The Internet Idea Book

The Internet Idea Book

101 Internet Business Ideas for the Everyday Ordinary Person

Michelle McGarry

Writers Club Press
San Jose New York Lincoln Shanghai

The Internet Idea Book
101 Internet Business Ideas for the Everyday Ordinary Person

Writers Club Press
an imprint of iUniverse.com, Inc.

For information address:
iUniverse.com, Inc.
620 North 48th Street, Suite 201
Lincoln, NE 68504-3467
www.iuniverse.com

The author does not guarantee success with any of the Internet business ideas in this book.

ISBN: 0-595-14437-3

Printed in the United States of America

Contents

To my husband, who has the patience to listen to all of my wacky ideas.

Introduction

The Internet is booming, there is not doubt about it. But so is the small- and home-business market, which emerged as a legitimate, profitable, and attractive enterprise at about the same time that the Internet began to gain popularity. Many people want to gain more control over their lives by starting their own business, and the Internet has opened the door to many more people who thought that starting their own business was a faint dream. This book is simply a collection of brainstorms, ideas of the kinds of businesses that could be started on the Internet, mostly for the home-based individual, such as the at-home parent, the student, the career-changer, or the retiree. But you will find that the descriptions are short for the most part. The other side of the process is yours: You must brainstorm your own ideas as well. Each idea is followed by a series of questions to answer, in workbook format, so that you can let your own imagination soar and design a site that is all yours.

I emphasize *niches* a lot in this book. I really believe that the Internet has opened doors for the individual entrepreneur, the everyday, ordinary person sitting at home in their living room wondering how they can make it on their own. But how do you compete with the huge companies creating huge Web sites laden with moving and talking graphics and high-tech HTML, run by large staffs of whiz kids? You don't. But the Internet has created opportunities for niches in the marketplace, more than ever existed in the traditional small business market before. The Web is publishing essentially, without the cost of paper and postage, and anyone with some meaningful information and basic computer skills can share that information with the rest of the world—literally. But as much as you can contact the entire world with your information, you can also contact your local communities more easily and quickly than ever before. There are millions of ways to target a business in this book to your local community, and millions more to target an idea to your own interests, skills, and energies. Part of the goal of this book is to get you to think about what your own dreams are, and how those dreams can fit into the needs of others. To that end, I have put together a list of other books that do a great job of getting you to explore what kind of business will work best for you. (See "Recommended Resources" at the end of the introduction.)

This book is organized by idea, with a short description of each one. Each idea is followed by a worksheet that is meant to get you to brainstorm for yourself how to put these ideas into action. I don't expect the whole book to be filled out. Rather, I expect that a few of the ideas in this book will get your imagination and your pen going. The worksheet is as follows:

Similar sites I've found online:

It's important to search the Web and research what other kinds of sites are out there that are similar to these ideas. Sites pop up every day, so this information can become outdated quickly. You also want to assess your competition and how you can target your site to compete effectively.

Special features I could add to this kind of site:

Brainstorm what features you could add to the site that would make it stand out. How can you make customer service better than your competitors? What marketing strategies would you employ? How would you keep track of your site visitors? What information or services will you add to the site that will make it more useful?

Niches I am interested in that could apply to this site:

This is the most important part of the worksheet. A successful Web site will be tailor-made for not only your audience, but also for *your* goals and dreams. You want to enjoy what you are doing, so you must pick a topic or business that you have a vested interest in. You also want to make money from your venture, so you must assess how your goals and dreams fit into the needs of others. Finding just the right niche in the marketplace can help you accomplish both. Finding a niche means narrowing your market. For example, say you want to create a Web site for doctors. A general site for doctors isn't very targeted. But, a Web site for pediatricians in the New York area who do housecalls: That is a specific niche. Brainstorm what niches and groups you are a part of, know a lot about, or have a lot of passion for. These types of niches will be the most enjoyable for you to work with and will help your site be successful because you have first-hand experience with them.

Income possibilities:

You also need to think about how you will make money from these ideas. Some ideas are more conducive to making money than others. On the Web, advertising is a primary source of income for many sites. You can also sell products on your site and make a profit that way. You can charge fees for services you provide on the Web. Perhaps you can sell subscriptions to a newsletter associated with your site, or create a paying membership of site visitors. You can also make commissions from affiliate programs when you promote products sold on other sites (see "Affiliate Web Site," p. 184). The ways in which you can make money from your site are limited only to your imagination.

Possible domain names for my site:

Finding the right domain name is important. A domain name is the name and address of your Web site (www.amazon.com; www.msn.com, etc.). What word(s) will you choose to describe your site's purpose? It should be something catchy and easy to remember. It shouldn't be too long (more than 15 characters). And, it has to be available. To check if someone else is not using your chosen domain name, go to any major online provider's Web site (such as mindspring.com) and simply check if your name is taken. If your name is taken, try the same name with a different extension than ".com." Dot-com names are the most popular and sought-after, but other extensions such as ".net" or ".org" can provide you with your desired descriptive words and are just as accepted as ".com."

Possible pitfalls:

With any business venture, you need to brainstorm what challenges you will face and how you can effectively deal with them. Sometimes even the most thought-out idea can have unforeseen problems. The only way to figure out which ideas will be most problematic is to research and test them. Make preliminary inquiries to vendors, survey your market, and do the preliminary work for the ideas that most appeal to you.

A rough sketch of how this site would be structured:

Use this blank space to sketch how your Web site might be organized. All sites start with a home page and then have links to subsequent pages. It helps to see how complex or simple your site will be before you begin constructing it. It will help you to visualize if you have chosen a niche that is too wide or too narrow.

It's important to remember that on the Web, there are unlimited possibilities, but site visitors do not have unlimited time. People don't have time for frivolous sites. The more Web sites that pop up, the less time people have to spend online, because there is simply too much information to look through. Choose carefully. Test your market. Follow through. Be consistent. And make your site worthy of our valuable time. Nothing is guaranteed! You need to do your own research and make your own judgments about these ideas. The success of any business depends on the efforts of the person who starts it, his or her drive to make it succeed, and of course, economic conditions and business feasibility.

Here are some tips to remember:

- Think local, or get specific on a national or international level.
- Individualize your effort. Do something only *you* can do, or that you can do better than anyone else.
- Read and research.
- Evaluate your strengths, opportunities, and drive.
- Find a niche and get as specific as you can without making your market too small.
- Think of a catchy, relevant domain name that attracts attention.
- Think of people you know and what types of services *they* would use or need on the Internet.
- None of these ideas are guaranteed moneymakers. They can be what you make of them.
- Follow your dream, but live the reality. Get the right angle on the dream you want to pursue, and nothing will stop you.

The Internet has opened up a wide world of possibilities for the everyday ordinary person who always dreamed of being an entrepreneur. But at the same time, it has developed a lot of competition, because if virtually anyone can create a Web site, you are in competition with most everyone. But then, you have something only you can offer and only you know what that is. So, explore my 101 Internet business ideas—use the workbook space and brainstorm how you can make these ideas even better, by tailoring them to *your* goals, interests, and dreams.

Recommended Resources

Finding Your Perfect Work: The New Career Guide to Making a Living, Creating a Life
by Paul Edwards and Sarah Edwards

Making Money with Your Computer at Home
by Paul Edwards and Sarah Edwards

The Best Home Businesses for the 90s: The Inside Information You Need to Know to Select a Home-Based Business That's Right for You
by Paul Edwards and Sarah Edwards

Clicking: 17 Trends That Drive Your Business and Your Life
by Faith Popcorn and Lys Marigold

Businesses You Can Start Almanac
by Katina Jones

Guerrilla Marketing Online: The Entrepreneur's Guide to Earning Profits on the Internet
by Jay Conrad Levinson and Charles Rubin

Guerrilla Marketing With Technology: Unleashing the Full Potential of Your Small Business
by Jay Conrad Levinson

Wholesale by Mail and Online 2000
by the Print Project

Do What You Love, the Money Will Follow: Discovering Your Right Livelihood
by Marsha Sinetar
Do What You Are: Discover the Perfect Career for You Through the Secrets of Personality Type
by Paul D. Tieger and Barbara Barron-Tieger

www.itoolbox.com
For the true beginner on the Internet, visit *itoolbox.com*, which sells the Internet Business Toolbox, an online kit that helps you develop and build an online business from soup to nuts.

1

Local Gift Certificates

Gift certificates are a great gift. Why not create a Web site where you sell gift certificates from local stores? The stores could pay a fee to participate in the service. Customers benefit from a site like this because it is a one-stop-shop where you can get certificates from specialty online stores or local stores that they might not normally have access to. Target the site to specific stores; say from a local area, or to a specific market. How about gift certificates to beauty salons or day spas for wedding day makeovers? Compare your ideas to a big site like—what else—*giftcertificates.com.*

Similar sites I've found online:

_____
_____
_____
_____
_____
_____
_____
_____
_____

Special features I could add to this kind of site:

_____

_____

_____

_____

_____

_____

_____

Niches I am interested in that could apply to this site:

_____

_____

_____

_____

_____

_____

_____

Income possibilities:

_____

_____

_____

_____

_____

_____

_____

Possible domain names for my site:

_____

_____

_____

_____

_____

_____

_____

_____

_____

Possible pitfalls:

_____

_____

_____

_____

_____

_____

_____

_____

A rough sketch of how this site would be structured:

2

Lunch Specials

Engage the participation of local restaurants to list their daily lunch specials on your Web site. The restaurants could pay a monthly fee to list their specials. Then market the site to local businesses. It's an inexpensive way for local restaurants to advertise and an easy, fast way for customers to browse what's for lunch each day. Be sure and talk to restaurant owners before you go ahead with this idea. Many restaurants may not plan their lunch specials ahead of time, or they may not have lunch specials at all.

Similar sites I've found online:

_____
_____
_____
_____
_____
_____
_____
_____
_____
_____

Special features I could add to this kind of site:

_____
_____
_____
_____
_____
_____
_____
_____

Niches I am interested in that could apply to this site:

_____
_____
_____
_____
_____
_____
_____
_____

Income possibilities:

_____
_____
_____
_____
_____
_____
_____
_____

Possible domain names for my site:

_____
_____
_____
_____
_____
_____
_____
_____

Possible pitfalls:

_____
_____
_____
_____
_____
_____
_____

A rough sketch of how this site would be structured:

3

Yard Sales

Create a site to list and promote local yard sales. Promote your site to potential advertisers and visitors through low-cost classified ads in local newspapers. Charge yard-sale owners a small fee to list their sales. Update the site weekly. This site is only good during fair weather months, typically May through October, depending on your locale. You can specialize in moving sales, estate sales, or yard and garage sales in your local area. You could also start an e-mail newsletter to keep track of visitors.

Similar sites I've found online:

_____
_____
_____
_____
_____
_____
_____
_____
_____
_____

Special features I could add to this kind of site:

_____

_____

_____

_____

_____

_____

_____

_____

Niches I am interested in that could apply to this site:

_____

_____

_____

_____

_____

_____

_____

_____

Income possibilities:

_____

_____

_____

_____

_____

_____

_____

_____

Possible domain names for my site:

_____

_____

_____

_____

_____

_____

_____

_____

Possible pitfalls:

_____

_____

_____

_____

_____

_____

_____

_____

A rough sketch of how this site would be structured:

4

Niche Classifieds

Classifieds are abundant on the Web, and many are free for advertisers, so you must create a site worthy of paying for. The answer? A solid niche. Work locally, or from a group that you are a part of or know a lot about. Also choose a group that readily uses the Internet. Charge advertisers to make your money, or charge a subscription rate to viewers if your content is juicy. Specializations are limited only to your imagination. Niches I've thought of include: College Student Classifieds; Your Profession's Classifieds; or Local Moms Classifieds.

Similar sites I've found online:

_____

_____

_____

_____

_____

_____

_____

_____

_____

_____

Special features I could add to this kind of site:

_____
_____
_____
_____
_____
_____
_____
_____

Niches I am interested in that could apply to this site:

_____
_____
_____
_____
_____
_____
_____
_____

Income possibilities:

_____
_____
_____
_____
_____
_____
_____
_____

Possible domain names for my site:

_____

_____

_____

_____

_____

_____

_____

_____

Possible pitfalls:

_____

_____

_____

_____

_____

_____

_____

_____

A rough sketch of how this site would be structured:

5

Long Lost

The world is full of people who, for various reasons, have lost track of loved ones. Create a site devoted to posting messages for those trying to find one another. The site could feature a good search engine where people search for messages. E-mail alerts could be put in place for responses to messages. Possible markets include adoptees and birth parents, lost loves, old friends, and reunion-missing-in-actions. However, some subjects are taboo to make a living from, such as runaways, kidnapping victims, and missing persons. These subjects should be approached with care.

Similar sites I've found online:

_____
_____
_____
_____
_____
_____
_____
_____
_____
_____
_____

Special features I could add to this kind of site:

_____

_____

_____

_____

_____

_____

_____

_____

Niches I am interested in that could apply to this site:

_____

_____

_____

_____

_____

_____

_____

_____

Income possibilities:

_____

_____

_____

_____

_____

_____

_____

_____

Possible domain names for my site:

_____

_____

_____

_____

_____

_____

_____

_____

Possible pitfalls:

_____

_____

_____

_____

_____

_____

_____

_____

A rough sketch of how this site would be structured:

6

Your Town Secretary

Create a site to aid secretaries and executive assistants with many aspects of their jobs, such as meeting planning, travel planning, office management, and business services. Then, get advertisers such as local caterers, travel agents, cab and limo companies, banquet halls, meeting planners, temporary agencies, copy shops, computer services, office supply retailers, and restaurants, just to name a few. Feature online chat rooms for secretaries to vent, network, and get help. Advice columns and articles can help with office politics and with time and stress management. Feature a "help-wanted" and "work-sought" section.

Similar sites I've found online:

_____

_____

_____

_____

_____

_____

_____

_____

_____

_____

Special features I could add to this kind of site:

_____
_____
_____
_____
_____
_____
_____
_____

Niches I am interested in that could apply to this site:

_____
_____
_____
_____
_____
_____
_____
_____

Income possibilities:

_____
_____
_____
_____
_____
_____
_____
_____

Possible domain names for my site:

_____
_____
_____
_____
_____
_____
_____
_____
_____

Possible pitfalls:

_____
_____
_____
_____
_____
_____
_____
_____

A rough sketch of how this site would be structured:

7

Contest Crazy

Organize the menagerie of contests that bombard us every day. This type of site could generate income by advertising from the organizations running the contests or from subscriptions from site visitors. Go to local malls regularly to list all the local contests; choose only free entries. Go through daily newspapers, watch television commercials, and go food and mall shopping often. A special feature might be online registration for the participating contests.

Similar sites I've found online:

_____
_____
_____
_____
_____
_____
_____
_____
_____
_____

Special features I could add to this kind of site:

_____
_____
_____
_____
_____
_____
_____
_____

Niches I am interested in that could apply to this site:

_____
_____
_____
_____
_____
_____
_____
_____

Income possibilities:

_____
_____
_____
_____
_____
_____
_____
_____

Possible domain names for my site:

_____

_____

_____

_____

_____

_____

_____

_____

Possible pitfalls:

_____

_____

_____

_____

_____

_____

_____

_____

A rough sketch of how this site would be structured:

8

Recipe Swapper

Swap recipes within a group on the Internet. Focus your niche by cuisine, by a group of people interested in cooking (like recipes for fire fighters), by course (desserts, appetizers, etc.), or by a specific diet restriction (like wheat-free recipes, for example). Enlist memberships for access to view recipes as well as to post them. Special features might include special interest sub-Webs, chat rooms, and online cooking instruction.

Similar sites I've found online:

_____
_____
_____
_____
_____
_____
_____
_____
_____
_____

Special features I could add to this kind of site:

_____
_____

_____
_____
_____
_____
_____
_____
_____

Niches I am interested in that could apply to this site:

_____
_____
_____
_____
_____
_____
_____

Income possibilities:

_____
_____
_____
_____
_____
_____
_____

Possible domain names for my site:

_____
_____
_____
_____

_____

_____

_____

_____

Possible pitfalls:

_____

_____

_____

_____

_____

_____

_____

_____

A rough sketch of how this site would be structured:

9

College Student Guide to Your Town

Do you live near a college community? A metropolitan area with a high concentration of colleges, such as Boston or New York, would be a huge Web site, but a small college town site would be manageable. Create a guide for college students that surpasses what travel or college guides can offer. Local advertisers would include restaurants and bars, grocery stores and pharmacies, and virtually every retailer near the college, such as local attractions, typing and copy services, tutoring services—the list is endless. Chat rooms and special interest bulletin boards could work really well on this kind of site.

Similar sites I've found online:

_____
_____
_____
_____
_____
_____
_____
_____
_____
_____

Special features I could add to this kind of site:

_____
_____
_____
_____
_____
_____
_____
_____

Niches I am interested in that could apply to this site:

_____
_____
_____
_____
_____
_____
_____

Income possibilities:

_____
_____
_____
_____
_____
_____
_____

Possible domain names for my site:

_____

_____

_____

_____

_____

_____

_____

_____

Possible pitfalls:

_____

_____

_____

_____

_____

_____

_____

_____

A rough sketch of how this site would be structured:

10

Teach a Class Online

Do you have a special skill that you could teach to others? Why not teach it online? First, develop a curriculum, like you would for a regular class. Then, assess how transferable it is to the Web. Is one-on-one demonstration necessary? Do you need to *show* a lot rather than *tell*? If it seems viable for the Web, place your lessons in a password-restricted site and charge a fee for "tuition" and access to the lessons. You could offer "class time" in live chat-classrooms with other students once a week. Students could get questions answered via e-mail.

Similar sites I've found online:

_____

_____

_____

_____

_____

_____

_____

_____

_____

_____

Special features I could add to this kind of site:

_____

_____

_____

_____

_____

_____

_____

_____

Niches I am interested in that could apply to this site:

_____

_____

_____

_____

_____

_____

_____

_____

Income possibilities:

_____

_____

_____

_____

_____

_____

_____

_____

Possible domain names for my site:

_____
_____
_____
_____
_____
_____
_____
_____
_____

Possible pitfalls:

_____
_____
_____
_____
_____
_____
_____
_____

A rough sketch of how this site would be structured:

11

Referral Service

This is a standard home business idea that can be applied online. Using a searchable database on a Web site eliminates the need for you to man the telephones, which is much less time consuming. Create a database of professionals who you would refer to customers who seek their services. Specialization possibilities are unlimited. Charge those who you refer a fee for being included in the database. Research the professional group you intend to refer, because many professions already have national associations with referral databases on the Web, which they already pay for in their membership fees.

Similar sites I've found online:

_____
_____
_____
_____
_____
_____
_____
_____
_____
_____
_____

Special features I could add to this kind of site:

_____

_____

_____

_____

_____

_____

_____

Niches I am interested in that could apply to this site:

_____

_____

_____

_____

_____

_____

_____

Income possibilities:

_____

_____

_____

_____

_____

_____

_____

Possible domain names for my site:

_____
_____
_____
_____
_____
_____
_____
_____

Possible pitfalls:

_____
_____
_____
_____
_____
_____
_____
_____

A rough sketch of how this site would be structured:

12

Out to Dinner

Enlist the participation of local restaurants to create a site where site visitors can make live, real-time dinner reservations online. This site may need some advanced HTML skills to create and update it. Features could include online menus and daily dinner specials. You could specialize in a type of restaurant cuisine, by location, or by prices. The success of this kind of site would depend on excellent communication between restaurant owners and you.

Similar sites I've found online:

_____

_____

_____

_____

_____

_____

_____

_____

_____

_____

Special features I could add to this kind of site:

_____
_____
_____
_____
_____
_____
_____
_____

Niches I am interested in that could apply to this site:

_____
_____
_____
_____
_____
_____
_____
_____

Income possibilities:

_____
_____
_____
_____
_____
_____
_____
_____

Possible domain names for my site:

_____

_____

_____

_____

_____

_____

_____

_____

Possible pitfalls:

_____

_____

_____

_____

_____

_____

_____

A rough sketch of how this site would be structured:

13

Gift Baskets

Gift baskets are a long-standing staple in the home business market. Putting your basket business on the Web is the next logical step. But you can vary it as well: Instead of your own baskets, why not list local gift-basket businesses for a fee? Or, list supplies for gift basket businesses. Or, start your own specialized gift basket business, say, based on your locale or a specialty of your own that no other competitor offers. There is lots of competition out there, so research your market, and choose what you will basket wisely.

Similar sites I've found online:

_____

_____

_____

_____

_____

_____

_____

_____

_____

_____

Special features I could add to this kind of site:

_____

_____

_____

_____

_____

_____

_____

_____

Niches I am interested in that could apply to this site:

_____

_____

_____

_____

_____

_____

_____

_____

Income possibilities:

_____

_____

_____

_____

_____

_____

_____

_____

Possible domain names for my site:

_____
_____
_____
_____
_____
_____
_____
_____

Possible pitfalls:

_____
_____
_____
_____
_____
_____
_____
_____

A rough sketch of how this site would be structured:

14

E-mail Reminders

Set up a site where members can be reminded of important dates, such as birthdays, anniversaries, and holidays. This could be popular with busy executives. You'll need a database program and an e-mail program to set up this kind of site.

Similar sites I've found online:

_____

_____

_____

_____

_____

_____

_____

_____

_____

_____

Special features I could add to this kind of site:

_____

_____

_____

_____

_____

_____

_____

_____

Niches I am interested in that could apply to this site:

_____

_____

_____

_____

_____

_____

_____

_____

Income possibilities:

_____

_____

_____

_____

_____

_____

_____

_____

Possible domain names for my site:

_____

_____

_____

_____

_____

_____

_____

_____

Possible pitfalls:

_____

_____

_____

_____

_____

_____

_____

_____

A rough sketch of how this site would be structured:

15

Greeting Card Sender

Set up an online service where you send greeting cards for busy people. Customers enter the dates, names, addresses, and occasions and pay by credit card. You then send out the cards in a timely fashion. There is even software made with which you can print someone's signature right on the card! Clients could include busy executives in a metropolitan area, or large companies interested in keeping up with personal marketing, public relations, and customer service.

Similar sites I've found online:

_____
_____
_____
_____
_____
_____
_____
_____
_____
_____
_____

Special features I could add to this kind of site:

_____
_____

_____

_____

_____

_____

_____

_____

Niches I am interested in that could apply to this site:

_____

_____

_____

_____

_____

_____

_____

Income possibilities:

_____

_____

_____

_____

_____

_____

_____

Possible domain names for my site:

_____

_____

_____

_____

_____

_____

_____

_____

Possible pitfalls:

_____

_____

_____

_____

_____

_____

_____

A rough sketch of how this site would be structured:

16

Used for Sale

Set up a site to sell used items. This site would work best with items that ship easily and inexpensively, so furniture might be hard to do. But the door is wide open to other used items, such as books, CDs, clothes, kitchen supplies—almost anything. Find something unique to set up a niche in the marketplace. Used books, CDs, and movies are already readily available on the Web, although if you specialize in say, vintage movies or a specific kind of book or music, you could compete that way. Visit local flea markets and yard sales to keep up inventory, or perhaps you already have access to a category of used items.

Similar sites I've found online:

_____
_____
_____
_____
_____
_____
_____
_____
_____
_____

Special features I could add to this kind of site:

_____

_____

_____

_____

_____

_____

_____

_____

Niches I am interested in that could apply to this site:

_____

_____

_____

_____

_____

_____

_____

_____

Income possibilities:

_____

_____

_____

_____

_____

_____

_____

_____

Possible domain names for my site:

_____

_____

_____

_____

_____

_____

_____

_____

Possible pitfalls:

_____

_____

_____

_____

_____

_____

_____

A rough sketch of how this site would be structured:

17

Your Town

What could be closer to home than your own town? Chances are there is already a Web site (or many) dedicated to your town, but what unique perspective can you bring to a site on the same topic? One geared towards tourists? A site for long-time residents or a welcome wagon site for brand-new residents? You could focus your site on entertainment in the town, or local events, or on the history of the town. The possibilities on how you can focus this kind of site are endless. Make the market clear and the information compelling, and where site visitors go, advertisers will follow. And, you may know many of them by first name.

Similar sites I've found online:

_____
_____
_____
_____
_____
_____
_____
_____
_____
_____

Special features I could add to this kind of site:

_____

_____

_____

_____

_____

_____

_____

_____

Niches I am interested in that could apply to this site:

_____

_____

_____

_____

_____

_____

_____

_____

Income possibilities:

_____

_____

_____

_____

_____

_____

_____

_____

Possible domain names for my site:

_____

_____

_____

_____

_____

_____

_____

_____

Possible pitfalls:

_____

_____

_____

_____

_____

_____

_____

_____

A rough sketch of how this site would be structured:

18

Your Favorite Hobby

Turn your favorite hobby into your online career. Just about anything you do as a hobby can have a following on the Web. Sewing or quilting? Model trains? Antique clock collecting? Chances are there are sites on your hobby already out there—research them and network with them. It's valuable to list other sites on your site, because it aids your visitors and they will trust your site as a source. Revenue possibilities include advertisers, newsletter subscriptions, affiliate commissions from items promoted on your site (see Affiliate Web site, p. 184), and from retail items sold.

Similar sites I've found online:

_____
_____
_____
_____
_____
_____
_____
_____
_____
_____

Special features I could add to this kind of site:

_____
_____
_____
_____
_____
_____
_____
_____

Niches I am interested in that could apply to this site:

_____
_____
_____
_____
_____
_____
_____
_____

Income possibilities:

_____
_____
_____
_____
_____
_____
_____
_____

Possible domain names for my site:

_____
_____
_____
_____
_____
_____
_____
_____
_____
_____

Possible pitfalls:

_____
_____
_____
_____
_____
_____
_____
_____

A rough sketch of how this site would be structured:

19

I'm an Expert in...

Similar to "Your Favorite Hobby" (see p. 52), this kind of site focuses on your expert knowledge in a particular area. You share your expertise and know-how via your Web site. The same revenue options exist, with exclusive add-ons that include fees for your online advice or even ongoing retainers/fees for consulting online.

Similar sites I've found online:

_____
_____
_____
_____
_____
_____
_____
_____
_____
_____

Special features I could add to this kind of site:

_____
_____
_____
_____

_____
_____
_____
_____

Niches I am interested in that could apply to this site:

_____
_____
_____
_____
_____
_____
_____

Income possibilities:

_____
_____
_____
_____
_____
_____
_____

Possible domain names for my site:

_____
_____
_____
_____
_____
_____

_____

_____

Possible pitfalls:

_____

_____

_____

_____

_____

_____

_____

_____

A rough sketch of how this site would be structured:

20

Calendar Service

Calendar services have been a long-time home business opportunity staple, and they are easily converted to the Web. In fact, the Web can establish your calendar service overnight. Keep track of local events and keep your clients informed for a fee. Check out a more detailed description of calendar services in Paul and Sarah Edwards' book, *Best Home Businesses for the 90s.*

Similar sites I've found online:

_____

_____

_____

_____

_____

_____

_____

_____

_____

_____

Special features I could add to this kind of site:

_____

_____

_____

_____
_____
_____
_____
_____

Niches I am interested in that could apply to this site:

_____
_____
_____
_____
_____
_____
_____

Income possibilities:

_____
_____
_____
_____
_____
_____
_____

Possible domain names for my site:

_____
_____
_____
_____
_____

_____

_____

_____

Possible pitfalls:

_____

_____

_____

_____

_____

_____

_____

_____

A rough sketch of how this site would be structured:

21

Local Rental Houses

Any type of real estate is a hot commodity. Houses for rent are always in demand, whether you live in a vacation or year-round community. Create a site where you list these local houses. You can charge an advertising fee to owners or a commission fee to either the owner or renter. Commissions would probably be more successful (and are typical) charged to the owner for vacation rentals and to the renter for year-round rentals. Specialize in a local area, or in a type of housing, or for a particular market of renters.

Similar sites I've found online:

_____

_____

_____

_____

_____

_____

_____

_____

_____

_____

Special features I could add to this kind of site:

_____
_____
_____
_____
_____
_____
_____
_____

Niches I am interested in that could apply to this site:

_____
_____
_____
_____
_____
_____
_____
_____

Income possibilities:

_____
_____
_____
_____
_____
_____
_____
_____

Possible domain names for my site:

_____
_____
_____
_____
_____
_____
_____
_____

Possible pitfalls:

_____
_____
_____
_____
_____
_____
_____
_____

A rough sketch of how this site would be structured:

22

Apartment Finders

Help renters find their ideal apartment—in the right neighborhood, at the right rent. High turnover areas, like college towns for example, would be good areas to begin a site like this. Or, areas where finding an apartment is a *bear* could be valuable too.

Similar sites I've found online:

_____
_____
_____
_____
_____
_____
_____
_____
_____

Special features I could add to this kind of site:

_____
_____
_____
_____
_____

_____

_____

_____

Niches I am interested in that could apply to this site:

_____

_____

_____

_____

_____

_____

_____

_____

Income possibilities:

_____

_____

_____

_____

_____

_____

_____

_____

Possible domain names for my site:

_____

_____

_____

_____

_____

_____

_____

_____

Possible pitfalls:

_____

_____

_____

_____

_____

_____

_____

A rough sketch of how this site would be structured:

23

Niche Directory

Are you part of a group that would benefit from having a directory of services on the Web? Any niche group would work—plumbers, home-care nurses, dentists, landscapers, nannies, or even clowns! Working on a local level, you can create a searchable database for site visitors to find exactly whom they need in your area. Members of the directory can pay a listing fee, and you could add on advertising rates for larger ads if you wish.

Similar sites I've found online:

_____
_____
_____
_____
_____
_____
_____
_____
_____
_____

Special features I could add to this kind of site:

_____
_____

_____
_____
_____
_____
_____
_____

Niches I am interested in that could apply to this site:

_____
_____
_____
_____
_____
_____
_____

Income possibilities:

_____
_____
_____
_____
_____
_____
_____

Possible domain names for my site:

_____
_____
_____
_____

_____

_____

_____

_____

Possible pitfalls:

_____

_____

_____

_____

_____

_____

_____

_____

A rough sketch of how this site would be structured:

24

Niche Yellow Pages

Similar to "Niche Directory" on p. 67, an online yellow pages is also a directory of services, but instead of focusing on a specific type of service, online yellow pages cover *everything* from A to Z. There are many online yellow pages, so you will need to select your niche carefully. Focusing locally may be the key for the individual entrepreneur to compete and so it doesn't get overwhelming.

Similar sites I've found online:

_____
_____
_____
_____
_____
_____
_____
_____
_____
_____

Special features I could add to this kind of site:

_____
_____
_____

_____

_____

_____

_____

_____

Niches I am interested in that could apply to this site:

_____

_____

_____

_____

_____

_____

_____

_____

Income possibilities:

_____

_____

_____

_____

_____

_____

_____

_____

Possible domain names for my site:

_____

_____

_____

_____

_____

_____

_____

_____

Possible pitfalls:

_____

_____

_____

_____

_____

_____

_____

_____

A rough sketch of how this site would be structured:

25

Online Newsletter

Create a newsletter in your specialty (or in a subject of your choosing) and promote and distribute it online. Most e-mail newsletters are free and meant to promote a business or Web site, so your newsletter should contain some pretty hefty information to get people to pay for a subscription. Find your niche and what they will pay for to know. Also check out the *Newsletter Sourcebook* by Mark Beach and Elaine Floyd and *Marketing with Newsletters: How to Boost Sales, Add Members & Raise Funds with a Printed, Faxed or Web-Site Newsletter* by Elaine Floyd.

Similar sites I've found online:

_____
_____
_____
_____
_____
_____
_____
_____
_____
_____

Special features I could add to this kind of site:

_____

_____

_____

_____

_____

_____

_____

_____

Niches I am interested in that could apply to this site:

_____

_____

_____

_____

_____

_____

_____

_____

Income possibilities:

_____

_____

_____

_____

_____

_____

_____

_____

Possible domain names for my site:

_____
_____
_____
_____
_____
_____
_____
_____

Possible pitfalls:

_____
_____
_____
_____
_____
_____
_____
_____

A rough sketch of how this site would be structured:

26

Jobs in Your Field

How often do you peruse the job listings in your field? Connect with other people like yourself. Employment listing Web sites are plentiful on the Web, but only a few have begun to specialize in particular kinds of jobs. Even fewer focus on a local area as well. Why not begin a site in your field, even in your own local area? Targeted sites like this one have great potential for a steady audience, and therefore valuable ad space.

Similar sites I've found online:

_____
_____
_____
_____
_____
_____
_____
_____
_____
_____

Special features I could add to this kind of site:

_____
_____
_____

_____
_____
_____
_____
_____

Niches I am interested in that could apply to this site:

_____
_____
_____
_____
_____
_____
_____
_____

Income possibilities:

_____
_____
_____
_____
_____
_____
_____
_____

Possible domain names for my site:

_____
_____
_____
_____
_____

_____

_____

_____

Possible pitfalls:

_____

_____

_____

_____

_____

_____

_____

_____

A rough sketch of how this site would be structured:

27

Advice Column

Do you have a unique perspective that you could bring to other people's problems? You could start your own "Dear Abby" site. Make it clear whether your advice is professional or just your opinion. Focus on a specific problem type (love problems, sex problems, family problems, etc.) or on your specific readership. A twist: What about visitors posting their problems and letting other visitors offer *their* advice?

Similar sites I've found online:

_____

_____

_____

_____

_____

_____

_____

_____

_____

_____

_____

Special features I could add to this kind of site:

_____

_____

_____

_____
_____
_____
_____
_____

Niches I am interested in that could apply to this site:

_____
_____
_____
_____
_____
_____
_____
_____

Income possibilities:

_____
_____
_____
_____
_____
_____
_____
_____

Possible domain names for my site:

_____
_____
_____
_____
_____

_____

_____

_____

Possible pitfalls:

_____

_____

_____

_____

_____

_____

_____

_____

A rough sketch of how this site would be structured:

28

Online Game

Do you have creative computer and HTML skills? You could design your own online (hopefully addictive) game. Players could pay a membership fee to play. The game is limited only to your imagination—from a simple card game like Hearts, to a popular group game like Bingo, to an interactive character game like "Dungeons & Dragons."

Similar sites I've found online:

_____

_____

_____

_____

_____

_____

_____

_____

_____

Special features I could add to this kind of site:

_____

_____

_____

_____

_____
_____
_____
_____

Niches I am interested in that could apply to this site:

_____
_____
_____
_____
_____
_____
_____
_____

Income possibilities:

_____
_____
_____
_____
_____
_____
_____
_____

Possible domain names for my site:

_____
_____
_____
_____
_____
_____

_____

_____

Possible pitfalls:

_____

_____

_____

_____

_____

_____

_____

_____

A rough sketch of how this site would be structured:

29

Local Products in Your Town

Find some unique shops in your local community and sell their products online for a commission. This site would be especially good in an area with some local flavor or distinctiveness. Particularly in smaller towns, local stores may jump at the chance to have their products marketed on an international level, without the responsibility of creating and running their own Web sites.

Similar sites I've found online:

_____
_____
_____
_____
_____
_____
_____
_____
_____
_____

Special features I could add to this kind of site:

_____
_____
_____

_____
_____
_____
_____
_____

Niches I am interested in that could apply to this site:

_____
_____
_____
_____
_____
_____
_____
_____

Income possibilities:

_____
_____
_____
_____
_____
_____
_____
_____

Possible domain names for my site:

_____
_____
_____
_____
_____

_____

_____

_____

Possible pitfalls:

_____

_____

_____

_____

_____

_____

_____

_____

A rough sketch of how this site would be structured:

30

Personal Ads

Create a site where people can find romance online. Personal ads are so popular in newspapers, they have the potential to flourish in a larger market on the Web. Target your site! The niche possibilities are endless, including by age, ethnic groups, sexual preferences, hobbies & interests, etc.

Similar sites I've found online:

_____

_____

_____

_____

_____

_____

_____

_____

_____

_____

Special features I could add to this kind of site:

_____

_____

_____

_____

_____
_____
_____
_____

Niches I am interested in that could apply to this site:

_____
_____
_____
_____
_____
_____
_____
_____

Income possibilities:

_____
_____
_____
_____
_____
_____
_____
_____

Possible domain names for my site:

_____
_____
_____
_____
_____
_____

_____

_____

Possible pitfalls:

_____

_____

_____

_____

_____

_____

_____

_____

A rough sketch of how this site would be structured:

31

Web Site Reviewer

Become an expert in a particular type of Web site and share your opinions with others. If you have expertise in Web design or as an editor, or in the subject of the sites you review, you will have good credibility.

Similar sites I've found online:

_____

_____

_____

_____

_____

_____

_____

_____

_____

_____

Special features I could add to this kind of site:

_____

_____

_____

_____

_____

_____

_____

_____

Niches I am interested in that could apply to this site:

_____

_____

_____

_____

_____

_____

_____

_____

Income possibilities:

_____

_____

_____

_____

_____

_____

_____

Possible domain names for my site:

_____

_____

_____

_____

_____

_____

Possible pitfalls:

_____

_____

_____

_____

_____

_____

_____

_____

A rough sketch of how this site would be structured:

32

Anything About Sex

Sex on the Internet is fast becoming a profitable industry. But I'd like to see some tasteful sites get some viewership also. Does it have to be pornographic to sell? I don't think so. You could have chat rooms on specific topics, sex advice (does Dr. Ruth have a site?), or even perhaps an online *Kama Sutra*.

Similar sites I've found online:

_____

_____

_____

_____

_____

_____

_____

_____

_____

_____

_____

Special features I could add to this kind of site:

_____

_____

_____

_____

_____
_____
_____
_____

Niches I am interested in that could apply to this site:

_____
_____
_____
_____
_____
_____
_____
_____

Income possibilities:

_____
_____
_____
_____
_____
_____
_____
_____

Possible domain names for my site:

_____
_____
_____
_____
_____
_____

_____

_____

Possible pitfalls:

_____

_____

_____

_____

_____

_____

_____

_____

A rough sketch of how this site would be structured:

33

Infomercial Junkie

I'm addicted to infomercials! Many people are. There are just so many products out there that seem to better our lives. Compile a site of information about infomercial products—either help promote them, or try them out and review them!

Similar sites I've found online:

_____
_____
_____
_____
_____
_____
_____
_____
_____
_____
_____

Special features I could add to this kind of site:

_____
_____
_____
_____
_____

_____

_____

_____

Niches I am interested in that could apply to this site:

_____

_____

_____

_____

_____

_____

_____

_____

Income possibilities:

_____

_____

_____

_____

_____

_____

_____

_____

Possible domain names for my site:

_____

_____

_____

_____

_____

_____

_____

Possible pitfalls:

_____
_____
_____
_____
_____
_____
_____
_____

A rough sketch of how this site would be structured:

34

For Sale by Owner

Many homeowners try to sell their own homes nowadays to avoid paying real estate agent fees. List FSBO homes in your local neighborhood for a small advertising fee. These sites are popping up all over, so check them out before you decide on your niche.

Similar sites I've found online:

_____
_____
_____
_____
_____
_____
_____
_____
_____
_____
_____
_____

Special features I could add to this kind of site:

_____
_____
_____
_____
_____

_____
_____
_____

Niches I am interested in that could apply to this site:

_____
_____
_____
_____
_____
_____
_____
_____

Income possibilities:

_____
_____
_____
_____
_____
_____
_____

Possible domain names for my site:

_____
_____
_____
_____
_____
_____
_____

_____

Possible pitfalls:

_____
_____
_____
_____
_____
_____
_____
_____

A rough sketch of how this site would be structured:

35

Online Dating Service

How many dating services are there out there? And how many stories have you heard about lovers meeting online? Now with emerging technology, videos can be viewed on the Web—a perfect forum for spouse shopping. Create an online dating service. Initial contacts could take place via e-mail rather than on a first date!

Similar sites I've found online:

_____
_____
_____
_____
_____
_____
_____
_____
_____
_____
_____

Special features I could add to this kind of site:

_____
_____
_____
_____

_____

_____

_____

_____

Niches I am interested in that could apply to this site:

_____

_____

_____

_____

_____

_____

_____

Income possibilities:

_____

_____

_____

_____

_____

_____

_____

Possible domain names for my site:

_____

_____

_____

_____

_____

_____
_____

Possible pitfalls:
_____
_____
_____
_____
_____
_____
_____
_____

A rough sketch of how this site would be structured:

36

Local Grocery Delivery

Some large grocery distributors have reinstated the convenient, old-fashioned grocery delivery service, but they have reinvented it online. Check out *peapod.com* or *homegrocer.com*. Are these services available in your neighborhood? If not, start one with your local grocer, or with your local fresh vegetable stand.

Similar sites I've found online:

_____

_____

_____

_____

_____

_____

_____

_____

_____

_____

Special features I could add to this kind of site:

_____

_____

_____

_____

_____
_____
_____
_____

Niches I am interested in that could apply to this site:

_____
_____
_____
_____
_____
_____
_____

Income possibilities:

_____
_____
_____
_____
_____
_____
_____

Possible domain names for my site:

_____
_____
_____
_____
_____
_____

_____
_____

Possible pitfalls:

_____
_____
_____
_____
_____
_____
_____
_____

A rough sketch of how this site would be structured:

37

Local Video Rental and Delivery

Pick-up and delivery of videotapes should be the next service offered for fanatic but busy moviegoers like myself. Charge the video stores to participate, or if you live in an affluent area with money to burn, charge the customers. Or, buy your own videos and create reels on wheels!

Similar sites I've found online:

_____

_____

_____

_____

_____

_____

_____

_____

_____

_____

_____

Special features I could add to this kind of site:

_____

_____

_____

_____

_____

_____

_____

_____

Niches I am interested in that could apply to this site:

_____

_____

_____

_____

_____

_____

_____

_____

Income possibilities:

_____

_____

_____

_____

_____

_____

_____

_____

Possible domain names for my site:

_____

_____

_____

_____

_____

_____

_____

Possible pitfalls:

_____
_____
_____
_____
_____
_____
_____

A rough sketch of how this site would be structured:

38

Anything For Rent and Delivery

Along the rental and delivery theme, *anything* for rent and delivery might succeed as an online business locally. Brainstorm some ideas!

Similar sites I've found online:

_____
_____
_____
_____
_____
_____
_____
_____
_____
_____
_____

Special features I could add to this kind of site:

_____
_____
_____
_____
_____
_____
_____

Niches I am interested in that could apply to this site:

Income possibilities:

Possible domain names for my site:

_____

Possible pitfalls:

_____
_____
_____
_____
_____
_____
_____

_____

A rough sketch of how this site would be structured:

39

Take a Tour

Promote local tours of your area online. Even lesser known vacation spots can gain popularity with more exposure on the Web. What is special about your area, and how much can you tell others about it?

Similar sites I've found online:

_____

_____

_____

_____

_____

_____

_____

_____

_____

_____

Special features I could add to this kind of site:

_____

_____

_____

_____

_____

_____

_____

_____

Niches I am interested in that could apply to this site:

_____

_____

_____

_____

_____

_____

_____

Income possibilities:

_____

_____

_____

_____

_____

_____

_____

Possible domain names for my site:

_____

_____

_____

_____

_____

_____

Possible pitfalls:

_____

_____

_____

_____

_____

_____

_____

A rough sketch of how this site would be structured:

40

Online Secretary

Create a reminder service for business travelers on the road: Help them wake up on time and remember the times and dates of business meetings. Many business travelers have online access on the road and can register their appointments online. Now with mobile Web services via cellular phones, you can set up a process whereby you send a reminder e-mail to your clients about meetings and it comes up on their cell phone.

Similar sites I've found online:

_____

_____

_____

_____

_____

_____

_____

_____

_____

Special features I could add to this kind of site:

_____

_____

_____
_____
_____
_____
_____
_____
_____

Niches I am interested in that could apply to this site:

_____
_____
_____
_____
_____
_____
_____

Income possibilities:

_____
_____
_____
_____
_____
_____
_____

Possible domain names for my site:

_____
_____
_____
_____

_____

_____

_____

_____

Possible pitfalls:

_____

_____

_____

_____

_____

_____

_____

_____

A rough sketch of how this site would be structured:

41

Speakers Bureau

Create a site where you promote and book speakers for special events. The Web is a great forum for this type of business because photographs, biographies, and even excerpts from previous speeches can add a lot to your speakers' profiles. Charge speakers a commission for bookings.

Similar sites I've found online:

_____

_____

_____

_____

_____

_____

_____

_____

_____

_____

Special features I could add to this kind of site:

_____

_____

_____

_____
_____
_____
_____
_____

Niches I am interested in that could apply to this site:

_____
_____
_____
_____
_____
_____
_____
_____

Income possibilities:

_____
_____
_____
_____
_____
_____
_____
_____

Possible domain names for my site:

_____
_____
_____
_____
_____

_____

_____

_____

Possible pitfalls:

_____

_____

_____

_____

_____

_____

_____

_____

A rough sketch of how this site would be structured:

42

Online Tutor

Offer online help for struggling students. Tutor students yourself or create a referral database for local tutors (see Referral Service, p. 31). Target your site in a particular academic subject or in your local area.

Similar sites I've found online:

_____

_____

_____

_____

_____

_____

_____

_____

_____

_____

Special features I could add to this kind of site:

_____

_____

_____

_____

_____

_____

_____

_____

Niches I am interested in that could apply to this site:

_____
_____
_____
_____
_____
_____
_____
_____

Income possibilities:

_____
_____
_____
_____
_____
_____
_____
_____

Possible domain names for my site:

_____
_____
_____
_____
_____
_____
_____

_____

Possible pitfalls:

_____
_____
_____
_____
_____
_____
_____
_____

_____

A rough sketch of how this site would be structured:

43

Stock Photos

Are you an amateur photographer? Stock photos are used all the time in magazines and books as filler, or as a cheaper alternative for cover and feature artwork. Take your own photos and sell them or rent their usage on the Web. A special feature could be downloadable, high resolution, ready-to-use images.

Similar sites I've found online:

_____
_____
_____
_____
_____
_____
_____
_____
_____
_____

Special features I could add to this kind of site:

_____
_____
_____
_____

_____
_____
_____
_____

Niches I am interested in that could apply to this site:

_____
_____
_____
_____
_____
_____
_____
_____

Income possibilities:

_____
_____
_____
_____
_____
_____
_____
_____

Possible domain names for my site:

_____
_____
_____
_____
_____

_____

_____

Possible pitfalls:

_____
_____
_____
_____
_____
_____
_____

_____

A rough sketch of how this site would be structured:

44

Online Critic

I would love to be a television critic. Is there something you have a lot to say about? Books, magazines, movies, television, the Web? Establish yourself as a respected critic of one of these medias.

Similar sites I've found online:

_____

_____

_____

_____

_____

_____

_____

_____

_____

_____

Special features I could add to this kind of site:

_____

_____

_____

_____

_____

_____
_____

Niches I am interested in that could apply to this site:

_____
_____
_____
_____
_____
_____
_____
_____

Income possibilities:

_____
_____
_____
_____
_____
_____
_____
_____

Possible domain names for my site:

_____
_____
_____
_____
_____
_____
_____

_____

Possible pitfalls:

_____

_____

_____

_____

_____

_____

_____

_____

A rough sketch of how this site would be structured:

45

Temporary Help

With an online temporary help site, you have the power to include biographies and resumes of your talented helpers. Specialize in a type of temp!

Similar sites I've found online:

_____
_____
_____
_____
_____
_____
_____
_____
_____
_____

_____

Special features I could add to this kind of site:

_____
_____
_____
_____
_____
_____

_____

_____

Niches I am interested in that could apply to this site:

_____

_____

_____

_____

_____

_____

_____

_____

Income possibilities:

_____

_____

_____

_____

_____

_____

_____

Possible domain names for my site:

_____

_____

_____

_____

_____

_____

_____

_____

Possible pitfalls:

_____
_____
_____
_____
_____
_____
_____
_____

A rough sketch of how this site would be structured:

46

Cubicle Relief

Create an outlet for those millions of people who identify with being trapped in a cubicle Monday through Friday. On a smaller level, target your site to workers in your own company or city. Create chat rooms, reviews of lunch spots and their specials, job listings, stress management tips, and more.

Similar sites I've found online:

_____

_____

_____

_____

_____

_____

_____

_____

_____

_____

Special features I could add to this kind of site:

_____

_____

_____

_____

_____
_____
_____
_____

Niches I am interested in that could apply to this site:

_____
_____
_____
_____
_____
_____
_____
_____

Income possibilities:

_____
_____
_____
_____
_____
_____
_____
_____

Possible domain names for my site:

_____
_____
_____
_____
_____
_____

_____

_____

Possible pitfalls:

_____
_____
_____
_____
_____
_____
_____

_____

A rough sketch of how this site would be structured:

47

Real Estate

There is no limit to the variety of real estate Web sites possible. (See "For Sale by Owner," p. 100; "Apartment Finders," p. 64; and "Million-Dollar Homes," p. 295). Scout your neighborhood for great houses and gather information about them from their real estate brokers. Or, charge advertising rates to brokers to list their houses themselves on your established, respected site. Use your imagination.

Similar sites I've found online:

_____

_____

_____

_____

_____

_____

_____

_____

_____

_____

_____

Special features I could add to this kind of site:

_____

_____

_____

_____

_____

_____

_____

_____

Niches I am interested in that could apply to this site:

_____

_____

_____

_____

_____

_____

_____

_____

Income possibilities:

_____

_____

_____

_____

_____

_____

_____

Possible domain names for my site:

_____

_____

_____

_____

_____

_____

_____

Possible pitfalls:

_____

_____

_____

_____

_____

_____

_____

_____

A rough sketch of how this site would be structured:

48

Online Coupons

How many coupon books do you get in the mail every week? Why not start your own coupon collections from local businesses on the Web? They're easy to update and you will save tons o' money on paper, printing, and postage. This is also a good add-on service to an existing Web site.

Similar sites I've found online:

_____

_____

_____

_____

_____

_____

_____

_____

_____

_____

Special features I could add to this kind of site:

_____

_____

_____

_____

_____
_____
_____
_____

Niches I am interested in that could apply to this site:

_____
_____
_____
_____
_____
_____
_____
_____

Income possibilities:

_____
_____
_____
_____
_____
_____
_____
_____

Possible domain names for my site:

_____
_____
_____
_____
_____
_____
_____

_____

_____

Possible pitfalls:

_____

_____

_____

_____

_____

_____

_____

_____

A rough sketch of how this site would be structured:

49

Local Art Broker

Do you live near an artist community? Or, do you have struggling-artist friends or family? The Internet is a wide-open marketplace for the sale of local art. You can open your own online gallery.

Similar sites I've found online:

_____
_____
_____
_____
_____
_____
_____
_____
_____
_____

Special features I could add to this kind of site:

_____
_____
_____
_____
_____
_____

_____

_____

Niches I am interested in that could apply to this site:

_____

_____

_____

_____

_____

_____

_____

_____

Income possibilities:

_____

_____

_____

_____

_____

_____

_____

_____

Possible domain names for my site:

_____

_____

_____

_____

_____

_____

_____

_____

Possible pitfalls:

_____
_____
_____
_____
_____
_____
_____
_____

A rough sketch of how this site would be structured:

50

Local Music Broker

Because it's easier than ever to create your own music CD, many struggling musicians are producing their own debut (and subsequent)
albums. Seek out some local talent and market their self-produced CDs
to a targeted audience for a commission. With Internet audio technology, you can have samples of the songs on the site for viewers to hear.
Also, don't forget to list the musicians' local live performances.

Similar sites I've found online:

_____

_____

_____

_____

_____

_____

_____

_____

_____

Special features I could add to this kind of site:

_____

_____

_____

_____
_____
_____
_____
_____

Niches I am interested in that could apply to this site:

_____
_____
_____
_____
_____
_____
_____

Income possibilities:

_____
_____
_____
_____
_____
_____
_____

Possible domain names for my site:

_____
_____
_____
_____
_____

_____
_____
_____

Possible pitfalls:

_____
_____
_____
_____
_____
_____
_____
_____

A rough sketch of how this site would be structured:

51

Summer Jobs

This site could be as broad or as targeted as you want it. High school students. College students. Specific local areas. Specific types of jobs. Brainstorm some possibilities.

Similar sites I've found online:

_____
_____
_____
_____
_____
_____
_____
_____
_____

_____

Special features I could add to this kind of site:

_____
_____
_____
_____
_____
_____

_____

_____

Niches I am interested in that could apply to this site:

_____

_____

_____

_____

_____

_____

_____

_____

Income possibilities:

_____

_____

_____

_____

_____

_____

_____

Possible domain names for my site:

_____

_____

_____

_____

_____

_____

_____

_____

Possible pitfalls:

_____
_____
_____
_____
_____
_____
_____

_____

A rough sketch of how this site would be structured:

52

A Group You Belong To

See also "Your Favorite Hobby," p. 52 and "I'm an Expert in..." p. 55.
Brainstorm what groups you belong to and how you could apply one or
more to a Web site.

Similar sites I've found online:

_____

_____

_____

_____

_____

_____

_____

_____

_____

_____

Special features I could add to this kind of site:

_____

_____

_____

_____

_____

_____

_____

_____

Niches I am interested in that could apply to this site:

_____

_____

_____

_____

_____

_____

_____

_____

Income possibilities:

_____

_____

_____

_____

_____

_____

_____

_____

Possible domain names for my site:

_____

_____

_____

_____

_____

_____

_____

Possible pitfalls:

_____

_____

_____

_____

_____

_____

_____

A rough sketch of how this site would be structured:

53

Support Group

What subject do you have sympathy for? What kind of group are *you* looking for to share concerns and emotions with? Create your own online support group. Perhaps enlist the volunteer services of a professional to offer weekly online counseling. Chat rooms offer the opportunity for virtual interactive "group counseling."

Similar sites I've found online:

_____
_____
_____
_____
_____
_____
_____
_____
_____
_____
_____

Special features I could add to this kind of site:

_____
_____
_____
_____

_____
_____
_____
_____

Niches I am interested in that could apply to this site:

_____
_____
_____
_____
_____
_____
_____
_____

Income possibilities:

_____
_____
_____
_____
_____
_____
_____
_____

Possible domain names for my site:

_____
_____
_____
_____
_____

_____

_____

Possible pitfalls:

_____

_____

_____

_____

_____

_____

_____

_____

A rough sketch of how this site would be structured:

54

Take a Local Class

See also "Teach a Class Online," p. 28 and "Calendar Service," p. 58. List local classes from community centers, colleges, and adult education programs. Charge the schools ad rates for listings or pursue regular advertising. Offer online registration perhaps.

Similar sites I've found online:

_____

_____

_____

_____

_____

_____

_____

_____

_____

Special features I could add to this kind of site:

_____

_____

_____

_____

_____

_____

_____

_____

Niches I am interested in that could apply to this site:

_____

_____

_____

_____

_____

_____

_____

Income possibilities:

_____

_____

_____

_____

_____

_____

_____

Possible domain names for my site:

_____

_____

_____

_____

_____

_____

_____

_____

Possible pitfalls:

_____
_____
_____
_____
_____
_____
_____

_____

A rough sketch of how this site would be structured:

55

Local House Historian

Promote your services as a house historian, researching the history of past owners and their stories. Especially with older houses, some histories can be dramatic. Network with real estate agents to add clients. Add the history of your town to your site with the history of some of its more infamous houses.

Similar sites I've found online:

_____
_____
_____
_____
_____
_____
_____
_____
_____
_____

Special features I could add to this kind of site:

_____
_____
_____
_____

_____
_____
_____
_____

Niches I am interested in that could apply to this site:

_____
_____
_____
_____
_____
_____

Income possibilities:

_____
_____
_____
_____
_____
_____

Possible domain names for my site:

_____
_____
_____
_____
_____

_____

_____

Possible pitfalls:

_____

_____

_____

_____

_____

_____

_____

_____

A rough sketch of how this site would be structured:

56

Fundraisers

Create a place for organizations to promote their fundraisers, as well as a place for philanthropists to seek out tax-deductible donations. Or, help organizations think of new and creative ways to raise money.

Similar sites I've found online:

_____

_____

_____

_____

_____

_____

_____

_____

_____

Special features I could add to this kind of site:

_____

_____

_____

_____

_____

_____
_____

Niches I am interested in that could apply to this site:

_____
_____
_____
_____
_____
_____
_____
_____

Income possibilities:

_____
_____
_____
_____
_____
_____
_____
_____

Possible domain names for my site:

_____
_____
_____
_____
_____
_____

_____

Possible pitfalls:

_____
_____
_____
_____
_____
_____
_____

A rough sketch of how this site would be structured:

57

Craft Shows

Crafts are big business—just turn on the Home & Garden channel. List local craft shows, or host your own weekly show from local crafters. Get a commission from sales of crafts online, or sell advertising to the plethora of craft suppliers out there.

Similar sites I've found online:

_____
_____
_____
_____
_____
_____
_____
_____
_____
_____
_____

Special features I could add to this kind of site:

_____
_____
_____
_____
_____

_____
_____
_____
_____

Niches I am interested in that could apply to this site:

_____
_____
_____
_____
_____
_____
_____
_____

Income possibilities:

_____
_____
_____
_____
_____
_____
_____
_____

Possible domain names for my site:

_____
_____
_____
_____
_____
_____
_____

_____

Possible pitfalls:

_____
_____
_____
_____
_____
_____
_____

_____

A rough sketch of how this site would be structured:

58

Local Sales

Do you ever get overwhelmed with advertisements of what stores are having sales when? Stores pay big bucks to advertise their sales, so why wouldn't they add on a fee to list their sale on your Web site? The site could be a one-stop-shop for consumers to check where the best deals are each week.

Similar sites I've found online:

_____

_____

_____

_____

_____

_____

_____

_____

_____

Special features I could add to this kind of site:

_____

_____

_____

_____

_____

_____

_____

_____

Niches I am interested in that could apply to this site:

_____

_____

_____

_____

_____

_____

_____

_____

Income possibilities:

_____

_____

_____

_____

_____

_____

_____

_____

Possible domain names for my site:

_____

_____

_____

_____

_____

_____

_____

_____

Possible pitfalls:

_____

_____

_____

_____

_____

_____

_____

_____

A rough sketch of how this site would be structured:

59

Bargain Hunter

Do you love to seek out bargains? Create a site where you list the best prices and quality on different items in your town. You can cover *any-thing* from groceries to appliances to clothing. Or, specialize in a particular type of product like art supplies or beauty supplies.

Similar sites I've found online:

_____

_____

_____

_____

_____

_____

_____

_____

_____

Special features I could add to this kind of site:

_____

_____

_____

_____

_____

_____

_____

_____

Niches I am interested in that could apply to this site:

_____

_____

_____

_____

_____

_____

_____

_____

Income possibilities:

_____

_____

_____

_____

_____

_____

_____

_____

Possible domain names for my site:

_____

_____

_____

_____

_____

_____

_____

_____

Possible pitfalls:

_____
_____
_____
_____
_____
_____
_____
_____

A rough sketch of how this site would be structured:

60

Your Trade or Profession

What do you do for a living right now? Create a site for others who do what you do. What do people in your profession want and need? What do they spend money on? Brainstorm opportunities for income based on these needs.

Similar sites I've found online:

_____

_____

_____

_____

_____

_____

_____

_____

_____

_____

_____

Special features I could add to this kind of site:

_____

_____

_____

_____

_____
_____
_____

Niches I am interested in that could apply to this site:

_____
_____
_____
_____
_____
_____
_____

Income possibilities:

_____
_____
_____
_____
_____
_____
_____

Possible domain names for my site:

_____
_____
_____
_____
_____
_____
_____

_____

Possible pitfalls:

_____

_____

_____

_____

_____

_____

_____

_____

A rough sketch of how this site would be structured:

61

Sell a Product Online

The possibilities are endless when it comes to selling products online. What do you sell? Sell something that interests you, that is fairly inexpensive to ship, that is plentiful and available to you wholesale, and something that is useful and wanted. Check out *Wholesale by Mail and Online 2000* by the Print Project for ideas. See also "Sell Something Completely Wacky" on p. 268.

Similar sites I've found online:

_____

_____

_____

_____

_____

_____

_____

_____

_____

Special features I could add to this kind of site:

_____

_____

_____

_____
_____
_____
_____

_____

Niches I am interested in that could apply to this site:

_____
_____
_____
_____
_____
_____
_____

_____

Income possibilities:

_____
_____
_____
_____
_____
_____
_____

_____

Possible domain names for my site:

_____
_____
_____
_____
_____

_____

_____

_____

Possible pitfalls:

_____

_____

_____

_____

_____

_____

_____

_____

A rough sketch of how this site would be structured:

62

Affiliate Web Site

You can earn affiliate commissions from your site just by promoting an item sold on another site. For example, if you write about a book on your site, you can provide a special link to *amazon.com*'s Web site where visitors can then buy the book. When site visitors use this link and make a purchase, you earn a commission. The amount of the commission depends on the company who offers the affiliate program. Check out *linkshare.com* to register with many companies at once, like Hershey's Gift Shop, ESPN—the Store, and even American Express, to name just a few.

Similar sites I've found online:

_____

_____

_____

_____

_____

_____

_____

_____

_____

_____

Special features I could add to this kind of site:

_____
_____
_____
_____
_____
_____
_____
_____

Niches I am interested in that could apply to this site:

_____
_____
_____
_____
_____
_____
_____
_____

Income possibilities:

_____
_____
_____
_____
_____
_____
_____
_____

Possible domain names for my site:

_____

_____

_____

_____

_____

_____

_____

_____

_____

Possible pitfalls:

_____

_____

_____

_____

_____

_____

_____

_____

A rough sketch of how this site would be structured:

63

Local Wedding Services

Weddings are big business and Web sites about weddings abound. Compete with the larger sites by focusing on your local area and list their wedding services for a listing fee—everything from bakeries to florists to reception sites to justices of the peace. Get listings from online and mail order companies as well.

Similar sites I've found online:

_____
_____
_____
_____
_____
_____
_____
_____
_____
_____
_____

Special features I could add to this kind of site:

_____
_____
_____
_____

_____
_____
_____
_____

Niches I am interested in that could apply to this site:

_____
_____
_____
_____
_____
_____
_____

Income possibilities:

_____
_____
_____
_____
_____
_____
_____

Possible domain names for my site:

_____
_____
_____
_____
_____
_____

_____

_____

Possible pitfalls:

_____
_____
_____
_____
_____
_____
_____

_____

A rough sketch of how this site would be structured:

64

Part-time Work

Create a better place to find part-time work than the newspaper. List jobs available, or help place workers based on their skills and experience. Focus on a target group perhaps: high school students, at-home moms returning to work, or retirees for example.

Similar sites I've found online:

_____
_____
_____
_____
_____
_____
_____
_____
_____
_____

Special features I could add to this kind of site:

_____
_____
_____
_____
_____

_____

_____

_____

Niches I am interested in that could apply to this site:

_____

_____

_____

_____

_____

_____

_____

Income possibilities:

_____

_____

_____

_____

_____

_____

Possible domain names for my site:

_____

_____

_____

_____

_____

_____

Possible pitfalls:

_____
_____
_____
_____
_____
_____
_____

A rough sketch of how this site would be structured:

65

Yankee Swapper

Similar to "Used for Sale," p. 46—consider bartering for goods and services. Site visitors can trade their wares through your site. This is particularly useful on a local level. Check out *ubarter.com* and brainstorm how you could create a similar site.

Similar sites I've found online:

_____

_____

_____

_____

_____

_____

_____

_____

_____

_____

Special features I could add to this kind of site:

_____

_____

_____

_____

_____

_____

_____

Niches I am interested in that could apply to this site:

_____

_____

_____

_____

_____

_____

_____

_____

Income possibilities:

_____

_____

_____

_____

_____

_____

_____

_____

Possible domain names for my site:

_____

_____

_____

_____

_____

_____

_____

_____

Possible pitfalls:

_____

_____

_____

_____

_____

_____

_____

_____

A rough sketch of how this site would be structured:

66

Online Community

Create your own online world. What community most interests you of all that you belong to? The possibilities are endless.

Similar sites I've found online:

_____
_____
_____
_____
_____
_____
_____
_____
_____

_____

Special features I could add to this kind of site:

_____
_____
_____
_____
_____
_____

Niches I am interested in that could apply to this site:

_____
_____
_____
_____
_____
_____
_____
_____

Income possibilities:

_____
_____
_____
_____
_____
_____
_____

Possible domain names for my site:

_____
_____
_____
_____
_____
_____
_____

_____

Possible pitfalls:

_____

_____

_____

_____

_____

_____

_____

_____

A rough sketch of how this site would be structured:

67

Ideas for Sale

Do you have a lot of ideas on a particular subject? Share your ideas with others online for a subscription fee. Simple brainstorming could help someone finish a project or start a business—and you could get paid for the idea.

Similar sites I've found online:

_____
_____
_____
_____
_____
_____
_____
_____
_____
_____

Special features I could add to this kind of site:

_____
_____
_____
_____
_____

_____

_____

_____

Niches I am interested in that could apply to this site:

_____

_____

_____

_____

_____

_____

_____

Income possibilities:

_____

_____

_____

_____

_____

_____

_____

Possible domain names for my site:

_____

_____

_____

_____

_____

_____

Possible pitfalls:

_____

_____

_____

_____

_____

_____

_____

A rough sketch of how this site would be structured:

68

Online Creativity Consultant

The term "creativity consultant" was coined by Paul and Sarah Edwards (self-employment experts and authors) as a possible up-and-coming opportunity. Offer your creative services to others online. Or, network with others beginning this career and create a directory site (see p. 67) or database site (see p. 250). Read more about this possible opportunity in *Making Money With Your Computer at Home* by Paul and Sarah Edwards.

Similar sites I've found online:

_____

_____

_____

_____

_____

_____

_____

_____

_____

Special features I could add to this kind of site:

_____

_____

_____
_____
_____
_____
_____
_____
_____

Niches I am interested in that could apply to this site:

_____
_____
_____
_____
_____
_____
_____

Income possibilities:

_____
_____
_____
_____
_____
_____
_____

Possible domain names for my site:

_____
_____
_____
_____

_____

_____

_____

_____

Possible pitfalls:

_____

_____

_____

_____

_____

_____

_____

_____

A rough sketch of how this site would be structured:

69

Hear Live Local Music

Help local music-lovers stay on top of who's playing where and what the cover charge is. Offer bios of musicians and perhaps even sound-bytes of music. Charge the restaurants, bars, and clubs a listing fee because after all, they benefit from the customers you bring in. See also "Local Music Broker," p. 148.

Similar sites I've found online:

_____

_____

_____

_____

_____

_____

_____

_____

_____

_____

Special features I could add to this kind of site:

_____

_____

_____

_____

_____

_____

_____

_____

Niches I am interested in that could apply to this site:

_____

_____

_____

_____

_____

_____

_____

Income possibilities:

_____

_____

_____

_____

_____

_____

_____

Possible domain names for my site:

_____

_____

_____

_____

_____

_____

_____

Possible pitfalls:

_____

_____

_____

_____

_____

_____

_____

_____

A rough sketch of how this site would be structured:

70

Your Town Baby

Next to wedding services, baby products are big business too. Create a site that lists all the baby services, products, and resources in your community. Charge listing fees for advertising for local services, including diaper services, breastfeeding help, play groups, pediatricians, ob/gyns, nannies, carpools, and more.

Similar sites I've found online:

_____
_____
_____
_____
_____
_____
_____
_____
_____
_____

Special features I could add to this kind of site:

_____
_____
_____
_____

_____

_____

_____

_____

Niches I am interested in that could apply to this site:

_____

_____

_____

_____

_____

_____

_____

_____

Income possibilities:

_____

_____

_____

_____

_____

_____

_____

_____

Possible domain names for my site:

_____

_____

_____

_____

_____

_____

_____

_____

Possible pitfalls:

_____
_____
_____
_____
_____
_____
_____

_____

A rough sketch of how this site would be structured:

71

Events in Your Specialty

Create an online specialty calendar service that keeps track of conferences, classes, conventions, trade shows and other events in whatever your hobby or career is. Keep others in your interest group informed and up-to-date. Perhaps even offer online registration.

Similar sites I've found online:

_____

_____

_____

_____

_____

_____

_____

_____

_____

_____

Special features I could add to this kind of site:

_____

_____

_____

_____

_____

_____

_____

_____

Niches I am interested in that could apply to this site:

_____

_____

_____

_____

_____

_____

_____

_____

Income possibilities:

_____

_____

_____

_____

_____

_____

_____

Possible domain names for my site:

_____

_____

_____

_____

_____

_____

Possible pitfalls:

_____

_____

_____

_____

_____

_____

_____

A rough sketch of how this site would be structured:

72

Advocate

What is your personal mission? Is there one topic you'd love to be an advocate for? Find something you are passionate about and become an advocate online.

Similar sites I've found online:

_____

_____

_____

_____

_____

_____

_____

_____

_____

_____

Special features I could add to this kind of site:

_____

_____

_____

_____

_____

_____

_____

_____

Niches I am interested in that could apply to this site:

_____
_____
_____
_____
_____
_____
_____

_____

Income possibilities:

_____
_____
_____
_____
_____
_____
_____

_____

Possible domain names for my site:

_____
_____
_____
_____
_____
_____
_____

_____

Possible pitfalls:

_____
_____
_____
_____
_____
_____
_____

_____

A rough sketch of how this site would be structured:

73

Virtual Community Center

Do everything that a community center would do—without the walls. Post community events, begin adult or child sports leagues, organize fundraising events, plan trips. Create the source for community information in your neighborhood on the Web.

Similar sites I've found online:

_____

_____

_____

_____

_____

_____

_____

_____

_____

_____

_____

Special features I could add to this kind of site:

_____

_____

_____

_____

_____

_____

_____

_____

Niches I am interested in that could apply to this site:

_____

_____

_____

_____

_____

_____

_____

_____

Income possibilities:

_____

_____

_____

_____

_____

_____

_____

_____

Possible domain names for my site:

_____

_____

_____

_____

_____

_____

Possible pitfalls:

A rough sketch of how this site would be structured:

74

The Best of ...

Pick a topic of interest to you and be its personal recommendation service. The best restaurants of your town? The best of quilting books? The best of kids television? The best of sports equipment? Become *the* resource of whatever subject you pick.

Similar sites I've found online:

_____

_____

_____

_____

_____

_____

_____

_____

_____

_____

_____

Special features I could add to this kind of site:

_____

_____

_____

_____

_____

_____

_____

_____

Niches I am interested in that could apply to this site:

_____

_____

_____

_____

_____

_____

_____

_____

Income possibilities:

_____

_____

_____

_____

_____

_____

_____

_____

Possible domain names for my site:

_____

_____

_____

_____

_____

_____

_____

_____

Possible pitfalls:

_____
_____
_____
_____
_____
_____
_____

_____

A rough sketch of how this site would be structured:

75

Back to School

Know anyone what wants to go back to school? Create the authoritative source of college programs in your area. Include links to the schools' Web sites, as well as links to sites about particular majors, and to big college sites like *petersons.com*.

Similar sites I've found online:

_____
_____
_____
_____
_____
_____
_____
_____
_____
_____
_____

Special features I could add to this kind of site:

_____
_____
_____
_____
_____

_____

_____

_____

Niches I am interested in that could apply to this site:

_____

_____

_____

_____

_____

_____

_____

_____

Income possibilities:

_____

_____

_____

_____

_____

_____

_____

_____

Possible domain names for my site:

_____

_____

_____

_____

_____

_____

_____

_____

Possible pitfalls:

_____

_____

_____

_____

_____

_____

_____

_____

A rough sketch of how this site would be structured:

76

From Kitchen to Classroom

Target a back-to-school site for at-home moms going back to college. Create a supportive community for these moms to interact, accomplish their goals, and vent their frustrations.

Similar sites I've found online:

_____

_____

_____

_____

_____

_____

_____

_____

_____

_____

Special features I could add to this kind of site:

_____

_____

_____

_____

_____

_____

_____

_____

Niches I am interested in that could apply to this site:

_____

_____

_____

_____

_____

_____

_____

_____

Income possibilities:

_____

_____

_____

_____

_____

_____

_____

_____

Possible domain names for my site:

_____

_____

_____

_____

_____

_____

_____

_____

Possible pitfalls:

_____

_____

_____

_____

_____

_____

_____

_____

A rough sketch of how this site would be structured:

77

Online Personal Shopper

There are so many sites to shop on the Web it's hard to know where the best deals and products are. Seek out the best products (pick a category of products perhaps) and then find the best prices. Become an online consumer guide.

Similar sites I've found online:

_____

_____

_____

_____

_____

_____

_____

_____

_____

_____

Special features I could add to this kind of site:

_____

_____

_____

_____

_____

_____

_____

_____

Niches I am interested in that could apply to this site:

_____

_____

_____

_____

_____

_____

_____

_____

Income possibilities:

_____

_____

_____

_____

_____

_____

_____

Possible domain names for my site:

_____

_____

_____

_____

_____

_____

_____

Possible pitfalls:

_____
_____
_____
_____
_____
_____
_____

_____

A rough sketch of how this site would be structured:

78

Vigilante Consumer

For the extremely frugal person with a social conscience? Find the best deals, or be on the lookout for the best products. Keep track of recall products or become a product tester. Read *Clicking* by Faith Popcorn and Lys Marigold to learn about how they coined the term "Vigilante Consumer" and what they predict about this trend that can enhance this idea.

Similar sites I've found online:

_____
_____
_____
_____
_____
_____
_____
_____
_____
_____

Special features I could add to this kind of site:

_____
_____
_____

_____
_____
_____
_____
_____

Niches I am interested in that could apply to this site:

_____
_____
_____
_____
_____
_____
_____
_____

Income possibilities:

_____
_____
_____
_____
_____
_____
_____
_____

Possible domain names for my site:

_____
_____
_____
_____
_____

_____

_____

_____

Possible pitfalls:

_____

_____

_____

_____

_____

_____

_____

_____

A rough sketch of how this site would be structured:

79

Online Professional Advice

Create a site that has all sorts of professionals who give online advice. Accountants, lawyers, and doctors are only a few of the advisors you could enlist. Create the site where if people have a question, they go to your site first.

Similar sites I've found online:

_____

_____

_____

_____

_____

_____

_____

_____

_____

_____

Special features I could add to this kind of site:

_____

_____

_____

_____

_____

_____

_____

_____

Niches I am interested in that could apply to this site:

_____

_____

_____

_____

_____

_____

_____

Income possibilities:

_____

_____

_____

_____

_____

_____

_____

Possible domain names for my site:

_____

_____

_____

_____

_____

Possible pitfalls:

A rough sketch of how this site would be structured:

80

On a Budget

Baby on a budget? Wedding on a budget? Travel on a budget? Home decorating, home improvement, commuting, Hawaiian vacations, automotive care, groceries, beauty products—the possibilities are endless. Or, create a general site where you offer money-saving advice for a particular market.

Similar sites I've found online:

_____

_____

_____

_____

_____

_____

_____

_____

_____

_____

Special features I could add to this kind of site:

_____

_____

_____

_____

_____

_____

_____

_____

Niches I am interested in that could apply to this site:

_____

_____

_____

_____

_____

_____

_____

_____

Income possibilities:

_____

_____

_____

_____

_____

_____

_____

Possible domain names for my site:

_____

_____

_____

_____

_____

_____

_____

_____

Possible pitfalls:

_____

_____

_____

_____

_____

_____

_____

_____

A rough sketch of how this site would be structured:

81

Errand Service

Create an errand service for your local community. Pick up dry clean-
ing, take movies back to the video store, run paperwork for local offices,
receive UPS and FedEx packages for working couples, walk dogs. What
is needed in your area?

Similar sites I've found online:

_____

_____

_____

_____

_____

_____

_____

_____

_____

_____

Special features I could add to this kind of site:

_____

_____

_____

_____

_____

_____

_____

_____

Niches I am interested in that could apply to this site:

_____

_____

_____

_____

_____

_____

_____

Income possibilities:

_____

_____

_____

_____

_____

_____

_____

Possible domain names for my site:

_____

_____

_____

_____

_____

_____

_____

Possible pitfalls:

_____

_____

_____

_____

_____

_____

_____

_____

A rough sketch of how this site would be structured:

82

Home Gardener

Share the homegrown tips on gardening that you have perfected down the years. This is good for gardeners who specialize in a specific type of plant, especially something unusual or exotic. Put your green-thumb know-how to work. See also "Homegrown," p. 274.

Similar sites I've found online:

_____
_____
_____
_____
_____
_____
_____
_____
_____
_____

Special features I could add to this kind of site:

_____
_____
_____
_____

_____
_____
_____

Niches I am interested in that could apply to this site:

_____
_____
_____
_____
_____
_____
_____
_____

Income possibilities:

_____
_____
_____
_____
_____
_____
_____

Possible domain names for my site:

_____
_____
_____
_____
_____
_____

_____

_____

Possible pitfalls:

_____

_____

_____

_____

_____

_____

_____

_____

A rough sketch of how this site would be structured:

83

Ticket Agent

Become an online ticket agent for concerts, sports events, and shows. Become a ticket broker for the big events (national teams and Broadway shows), or, offer a site for local ticketed events—local sports tournaments, concerts, and shows.

Similar sites I've found online:

_____
_____
_____
_____
_____
_____
_____
_____
_____
_____

_____

Special features I could add to this kind of site:

_____
_____
_____
_____
_____

_____

_____

_____

Niches I am interested in that could apply to this site:

_____

_____

_____

_____

_____

_____

_____

Income possibilities:

_____

_____

_____

_____

_____

_____

_____

Possible domain names for my site:

_____

_____

_____

_____

_____

_____

_____

_____

Possible pitfalls:

_____
_____
_____
_____
_____
_____
_____
_____

A rough sketch of how this site would be structured:

84

Subject Database Site

A database site covers a wide range of services that all serve one subject. Similar to a directory that focuses on say, florists, a database would cover a wider range of services, like wedding or funeral services, and list all pertinent companies, including florists. See examples of database sites at "Local Wedding Services, " p. 187, and "Your Town Baby," p. 208.

Similar sites I've found online:

_____

_____

_____

_____

_____

_____

_____

_____

_____

_____

Special features I could add to this kind of site:

_____

_____

_____

_____

_____
_____
_____
_____

Niches I am interested in that could apply to this site:

_____
_____
_____
_____
_____
_____
_____
_____

Income possibilities:

_____
_____
_____
_____
_____
_____
_____
_____

Possible domain names for my site:

_____
_____
_____
_____
_____
_____

_____

_____

Possible pitfalls:

_____

_____

_____

_____

_____

_____

_____

_____

A rough sketch of how this site would be structured:

85

Pen Pals

Help others get connected overseas. Create a site similar to a dating service where you match up people with similar interests and ages who would like to become pen pals. Of course, this will probably be done by e-mail, instead of snail mail.

Similar sites I've found online:

_____

_____

_____

_____

_____

_____

_____

_____

_____

Special features I could add to this kind of site:

_____

_____

_____

_____

_____

_____

_____

_____

Niches I am interested in that could apply to this site:

_____

_____

_____

_____

_____

_____

_____

_____

Income possibilities:

_____

_____

_____

_____

_____

_____

_____

_____

Possible domain names for my site:

_____

_____

_____

_____

_____

_____

_____

_____

Possible pitfalls:

_____

_____

_____

_____

_____

_____

_____

_____

A rough sketch of how this site would be structured:

86

Diary

Voyeurism has exploded on television and on the Web, and this site might intrigue visitors. Using screen names, visitors (or paying members, say) enter their journal or diary entries online—for others to view and read. They in turn can read the diaries of others. A live soap opera online?

Similar sites I've found online:

_____
_____
_____
_____
_____
_____
_____
_____
_____
_____

Special features I could add to this kind of site:

_____
_____
_____
_____

_____
_____
_____
_____

Niches I am interested in that could apply to this site:

_____
_____
_____
_____
_____
_____
_____

Income possibilities:

_____
_____
_____
_____
_____
_____
_____

Possible domain names for my site:

_____
_____
_____
_____
_____
_____

_____

_____

Possible pitfalls:

_____

_____

_____

_____

_____

_____

_____

_____

A rough sketch of how this site would be structured:

87

Catalog Crazy

I love mail-order catalogs. Create a site where you report on all the neat products that are available through these lively companies. Most of these companies are now expanded to the Web, so you can create links to their Web sites, and perhaps become a part of their affiliate programs. Be the resource for customers to search through many types of catalogs at once. And for those mail-order catalogs still not on the Web, there are opportunities to assist them online as well.

Similar sites I've found online:

_____

_____

_____

_____

_____

_____

_____

_____

_____

Special features I could add to this kind of site:

_____

_____

Niches I am interested in that could apply to this site:

Income possibilities:

Possible domain names for my site:

_____

_____

_____

_____

Possible pitfalls:

_____

_____

_____

_____

_____

_____

_____

_____

A rough sketch of how this site would be structured:

88

Office Lunch Service

Prepare and deliver lunches to local offices. Focus on everyday lunches or on specially created lunches for meetings. Online ordering makes this business easily accessible to customers.

Similar sites I've found online:

_____

_____

_____

_____

_____

_____

_____

_____

_____

_____

_____

_____

_____

Special features I could add to this kind of site:

_____

_____

_____

_____

_____

_____

_____

_____

Niches I am interested in that could apply to this site:

_____
_____
_____
_____
_____
_____
_____
_____

Income possibilities:

_____
_____
_____
_____
_____
_____
_____

Possible domain names for my site:

_____
_____
_____
_____
_____
_____

_____

_____

Possible pitfalls:

_____

_____

_____

_____

_____

_____

_____

_____

A rough sketch of how this site would be structured:

89

Lottery News

Keep track of the local or national lotteries so people have a better place to check their numbers than the newspaper. Perhaps even profile big winners. This site has great potential for a *large* number of visitors. Advertising would likely be a main source of income.

Similar sites I've found online:

_____

_____

_____

_____

_____

_____

_____

_____

_____

_____

Special features I could add to this kind of site:

_____

_____

_____

_____

_____

_____

_____

_____

Niches I am interested in that could apply to this site:

_____

_____

_____

_____

_____

_____

_____

Income possibilities:

_____

_____

_____

_____

_____

_____

_____

Possible domain names for my site:

_____

_____

_____

_____

_____

_____

_____

_____

Possible pitfalls:

_____
_____
_____
_____
_____
_____
_____

_____

A rough sketch of how this site would be structured:

90

Sell Something Completely Wacky

There are a couple of women in Kansas who now make a good living selling tumbleweeds on the Web. *Tumbleweeds!* The site began as a joke until they began receiving cash orders. Check out *www.prairietumble weedfarm.com* and see for yourself. What is all around you that you might be able to profit from online, even if it seems outrageous?

Similar sites I've found online:

_____

_____

_____

_____

_____

_____

_____

_____

_____

_____

_____

Special features I could add to this kind of site:

_____

_____

_____

_____

_____
_____
_____
_____

Niches I am interested in that could apply to this site:

_____
_____
_____
_____
_____
_____
_____
_____

Income possibilities:

_____
_____
_____
_____
_____
_____
_____

Possible domain names for my site:

_____
_____
_____
_____
_____
_____

_____

_____

Possible pitfalls:

_____

_____

_____

_____

_____

_____

_____

_____

A rough sketch of how this site would be structured:

91

Fact Checker

Do you have a knack for research? Create a site where you find out the information that others need to know. Or, since most fact-checkers are freelancers, you could also create a directory site or referral service especially for them.

Similar sites I've found online:

_____
_____
_____
_____
_____
_____
_____
_____
_____
_____

Special features I could add to this kind of site:

_____
_____
_____
_____
_____

_____

_____

_____

Niches I am interested in that could apply to this site:

_____

_____

_____

_____

_____

_____

_____

Income possibilities:

_____

_____

_____

_____

_____

_____

_____

Possible domain names for my site:

_____

_____

_____

_____

_____

_____

_____

_____

Possible pitfalls:

_____

_____

_____

_____

_____

_____

_____

_____

A rough sketch of how this site would be structured:

92

Homegrown

Similar to "Home Gardener," p. 244, which offers advice, sell your home-grown wares on the Web. What do you grow? Herbs, sprouts, flowers, or specialty plants—something that grows only in *your* neck of the woods.

Similar sites I've found online:

_____

_____

_____

_____

_____

_____

_____

_____

_____

_____

Special features I could add to this kind of site:

_____

_____

_____

_____

_____

_____

_____
_____

Niches I am interested in that could apply to this site:

_____
_____
_____
_____
_____
_____
_____
_____

Income possibilities:

_____
_____
_____
_____
_____
_____
_____
_____

Possible domain names for my site:

_____
_____
_____
_____
_____
_____

_____

_____

Possible pitfalls:

_____

_____

_____

_____

_____

_____

_____

_____

A rough sketch of how this site would be structured:

93

Web Flourishes

This is the online version of a clip-art service. Do you have a flair for HTML or as an artist? Create Web flourishes and images and sell or rent your online clip art for others to add to their Web sites.

Similar sites I've found online:

_____
_____
_____
_____
_____
_____
_____
_____
_____
_____

Special features I could add to this kind of site:

_____
_____
_____
_____
_____
_____

_____

_____

Niches I am interested in that could apply to this site:

_____

_____

_____

_____

_____

_____

_____

_____

Income possibilities:

_____

_____

_____

_____

_____

_____

_____

_____

Possible domain names for my site:

_____

_____

_____

_____

_____

_____

_____

Possible pitfalls:

_____

_____

_____

_____

_____

_____

_____

_____

A rough sketch of how this site would be structured:

94

Travel Agent

Are you a travel agent? Check out *travelocity.com* and brainstorm what you could do locally to compete with big sites like this one. Or, use your travel agent expertise and focus your services on cruises or a specific destination or European bus tours—almost anything.

Similar sites I've found online:

_____
_____
_____
_____
_____
_____
_____
_____
_____
_____

Special features I could add to this kind of site:

_____
_____
_____
_____

_____

_____

_____

Niches I am interested in that could apply to this site:

_____

_____

_____

_____

_____

_____

_____

_____

Income possibilities:

_____

_____

_____

_____

_____

_____

_____

_____

Possible domain names for my site:

_____

_____

_____

_____

_____

_____

_____

_____

Possible pitfalls:

_____

_____

_____

_____

_____

_____

_____

_____

A rough sketch of how this site would be structured:

95

Travel Destinations

You don't have to be a travel agent to *know* about travel. Be a resource for those seeking escape. Focus on a niche: a specific kind of destination (mountain vacations or tropical beaches, for example) or on a target market (families or singles, for example).

Similar sites I've found online:

_____
_____
_____
_____
_____
_____
_____
_____
_____
_____

Special features I could add to this kind of site:

_____
_____
_____
_____
_____

_____

_____

_____

Niches I am interested in that could apply to this site:

_____

_____

_____

_____

_____

_____

_____

_____

Income possibilities:

_____

_____

_____

_____

_____

_____

_____

Possible domain names for my site:

_____

_____

_____

_____

_____

_____

_____

_____

Possible pitfalls:

_____

_____

_____

_____

_____

_____

_____

_____

A rough sketch of how this site would be structured:

96

Online Personal/Life Coach

This is a fairly new, rapidly growing field of consulting. Help others live their lives according to their values and accomplish their goals. Find out more about what a personal/life coach does at *focusedlives.com*. How could you offer coaching online?

Similar sites I've found online:

_____
_____
_____
_____
_____
_____
_____
_____
_____
_____

Special features I could add to this kind of site:

_____
_____
_____
_____
_____

_____
_____
_____

Niches I am interested in that could apply to this site:

_____
_____
_____
_____
_____
_____
_____
_____

Income possibilities:

_____
_____
_____
_____
_____
_____
_____
_____

Possible domain names for my site:

_____
_____
_____
_____
_____
_____

_____

_____

Possible pitfalls:

_____

_____

_____

_____

_____

_____

_____

_____

A rough sketch of how this site would be structured:

97

Just for Kids

More and more, children are on the Web. Create a site with fun educational games or an interactive online tournament. Create a Web newsletter. Focus on a specific age group or gender perhaps.

Similar sites I've found online:

_____

_____

_____

_____

_____

_____

_____

_____

_____

_____

Special features I could add to this kind of site:

_____

_____

_____

_____

_____

_____

_____

Niches I am interested in that could apply to this site:

_____

_____

_____

_____

_____

_____

_____

_____

Income possibilities:

_____

_____

_____

_____

_____

_____

_____

_____

Possible domain names for my site:

_____

_____

_____

_____

_____

_____

_____

Possible pitfalls:

_____

_____

_____

_____

_____

_____

_____

_____

A rough sketch of how this site would be structured:

98

Astrology

Do personal astrology charts for a fee and list general horoscopes to promote your site. Put that secret hobby to work for you.

Similar sites I've found online:

_____
_____
_____
_____
_____
_____
_____
_____
_____
_____
_____

Special features I could add to this kind of site:

_____
_____
_____
_____
_____
_____

_____
_____

Niches I am interested in that could apply to this site:

_____
_____
_____
_____
_____
_____
_____
_____

Income possibilities:

_____
_____
_____
_____
_____
_____
_____
_____

Possible domain names for my site:

_____
_____
_____
_____
_____
_____

_____

_____

Possible pitfalls:

_____

_____

_____

_____

_____

_____

_____

_____

A rough sketch of how this site would be structured:

99

Million-Dollar Homes

Just for fun, keep track of the for-sale million-dollar homes you have always wanted to tour. Haven't you always wanted to go to those open houses? Do it. Then describe the experience online, with a photo of the outside of the house, its listing price, and all the garish details.

Similar sites I've found online:

_____

_____

_____

_____

_____

_____

_____

_____

_____

_____

Special features I could add to this kind of site:

_____

_____

_____

_____

_____

_____

_____

_____

Niches I am interested in that could apply to this site:

_____

_____

_____

_____

_____

_____

_____

_____

Income possibilities:

_____

_____

_____

_____

_____

_____

_____

_____

Possible domain names for my site:

_____

_____

_____

_____

_____

_____

_____

Possible pitfalls:

_____

_____

_____

_____

_____

_____

_____

_____

A rough sketch of how this site would be structured:

100

Just for Lefties

Left-handed people make up a small percentage of our population, but they represent a very large number of people collectively. Lefties constantly drown in a world of products made for the right-handed. Create a site dedicated to products and resources just for them. See how a New Zealand company, The Left Centre, has done just that at *www.lefty.co.nz/*.

Similar sites I've found online:

_____

_____

_____

_____

_____

_____

_____

_____

_____

_____

Special features I could add to this kind of site:

_____

_____

_____

_____
_____
_____
_____
_____

Niches I am interested in that could apply to this site:

_____
_____
_____
_____
_____
_____
_____

Income possibilities:

_____
_____
_____
_____
_____
_____
_____

Possible domain names for my site:

_____
_____
_____
_____
_____

_____
_____
_____

Possible pitfalls:
_____
_____
_____
_____
_____
_____
_____
_____

A rough sketch of how this site would be structured:

101

Online Entrepreneur

Last, but not least, create a Web site for others like you—people who are or would like to be online entrepreneurs. You could focus on a particular market like the Mother's Home Business Network (*www.mhbn.com*) or Entrepreneurial Parent (*www.en-parent.com*). Or, offer a site that ferrets out the business opportunities that are scams. Or, create a network of local entrepreneurs who want to trade services. As with all these ideas, there is no limit to what you can do.

Similar sites I've found online:

_____
_____
_____
_____
_____
_____
_____
_____
_____
_____

Special features I could add to this kind of site:

_____
_____

_____

_____

_____

_____

_____

_____

Niches I am interested in that could apply to this site:

_____

_____

_____

_____

_____

_____

_____

Income possibilities:

_____

_____

_____

_____

_____

_____

_____

Possible domain names for my site:

_____

_____

_____

_____

_____
_____
_____
_____

Possible pitfalls:

_____
_____
_____
_____
_____
_____
_____
_____

A rough sketch of how this site would be structured:

About the Author

Michelle McGarry is a writer and editor based in Boston, Massachusetts. She enjoys surfing the Internet and exploring home business opportunities. She is married and has two children.

Index

www.ingramcontent.com/pod-product-compliance
Lightning Source LLC
Chambersburg PA
CBHW051223050326
40689CB00007B/783